One Duck, Another Duck

by CHARLOTTE POMERANTZ
pictures by JOSE ARUEGO and ARIANE DEWEY

HARCOURT BRACE & COMPANY
Orlando Atlanta Austin Boston San Francisco Chicago Dallas New York
Toronto London

For Susan, Thomas, Louie,
and Benjamin — C.P.

For Ada
— J.A. and A.D.

This edition is published by special
arrangement with Greenwillow Books,
a division of William Morrow,
Publishers, Inc.

Grateful acknowledgment is made to
Greenwillow Books, a division of
William Morrow & Company, Inc. for
permission to reprint *One Duck,
Another Duck* by Charlotte Pomerantz,
illustrated by Jose Aruego and Ariane
Dewey. Text copyright © 1984 by
Charlotte Pomerantz; illustrations
copyright © 1984 by Jose Aruego and
Ariane Dewey.

Printed in the United States
of America

ISBN 0-15-300310-3

4 5 6 7 8 9 10   059   96   95   94

Danny and his grandmother went to the pond.

They saw a mother duck with her baby ducks behind her. Danny started to count them. "One duck, another duck, another duck, another duck..."

"No," said Grandmother. "You know how to count.
One, two, three, and so on.
Count them again."

The ducks came out from behind the tall grass.
Danny counted. "One duck, another duck...

Two ducks, another duck...

Three ducks, another duck...

Four ducks, another duck...

Danny looked and looked.

"Another duck?" he asked.

"No," said Grandmother. "It's a swan.
One swan is not enough to count.
But look...here come some more ducks.
You have counted five.
What comes next?"

Danny counted. "Six ducks, another duck...

Seven ducks, another duck...

Eight ducks, another duck...

Nine ducks," said Danny.

Danny and Grandmother watched the ducks go by.
"Another duck?" he asked.
"No," said Grandmother. "No more ducks."

"Look, Grandma, you are wrong."

"Ten ducks," said Danny. "One, two, three, four, five, six, seven, eight, nine, ten."
"Very good," said Grandmother.
"You can count to ten."

"Look, Grandma!
   Now there are enough swans to count."

Grandmother yawned.
"No, Danny, enough counting.
It is time to go home."

Danny smiled to himself.
"I know," he thought.
"I'll count the stars."